Media Literacy for Kids

Learning About
Primary Sources

by Nikki Bruno Clapper

Consultant: JoAnne DeLurey Reed
Librarian and Teacher

CAPSTONE PRESS
a capstone imprint

Pebble Plus is published by Capstone Press,
1710 Roe Crest Drive, North Mankato, Minnesota 56003
www.capstonepub.com

Editorial Credits
Gillia Olson, editor; Cynthia Della-Rovere, designer; Wanda Winch, media researcher;
Laura Manthe, production specialist

Library of Congress Cataloging-in-Publication Data
Clapper, Nikki Bruno.
  Learning about primary sources / by Nikki Bruno Clapper.
    pages cm. -- (Pebble plus. Media literacy for kids)
  Includes bibliographical references and index.
  Summary: "Introduces readers to primary sources. Includes a hands-on activity related to media literacy"--
Provided by publisher.
  ISBN 978-1-4914-6050-4 (library binding) -- ISBN 978-1-4914-6070-2 (ebook pdf)
1. History--Sources--Juvenile literature. 2. History--Research--Juvenile literature. 3. Information resources--
Juvenile literature. 4. Media literacy--Juvenile literature. I. Title.
  D16.C52 2016
  907.2--dc23   2015006647

Photo Credits
Anne S. K. Brown Military Collection, Brown University Library, 13; Bridgeman Images: Leemage/Private
Collection, 21; Capstone Studio: Karon Dubke, 17, 19; CriaImages.com: Jay Robert Nash Collection, 22 (bottom);
Dreamstime: Spotmatik, 9; NASA: Johnson Space Center, 5; The Richmond-Times Dispatch, cover (Titanic
newspaper article); National Archives and Records Administration: David M. Rubenstein Gallery, 11; Newscom:
ABACA/PAPhotos/Whyld Lewis, 15, akg-images/Marion Kalter, 22 (top), Photoshot/UPPA, 7; Shutterstock:
Action Sports Photography, cover (bottom left), David Smart, cover (top right), Donna Beeler, cover (soldier),
LiliGraphie, cover (br), mtkang, cover (frame bl)

Note to Parents and Teachers

The Media Literacy for Kids set supports Common Core State Standards related to
language arts. This book describes and illustrates primary sources. The images support
early readers in understanding the text. The repetition of words and phrases helps early
readers learn new words. This book also introduces early readers to subject-specific
vocabulary words, which are defined in the Glossary section. Early readers may need
assistance to read some words and to use the Table of Contents, Glossary, Read More,
Internet Sites, Critical Thinking Using the Common Core, and Index sections of the book.

Printed in China by Nordica.
0415/CA21500542
032015   008837NORDF15

Table of Contents

Like a Time Machine

What was it like to walk on the moon for the first time? This photograph can tell you. It is a primary source.

Astronaut Buzz Aldrin walking on the moon in 1969.

A primary source helps you find out about the past. It comes from someone who was part of history. A primary source is an original, not a copy.

Pages from the diary of Anne Frank. She and her family hid from the Nazis during World War II.

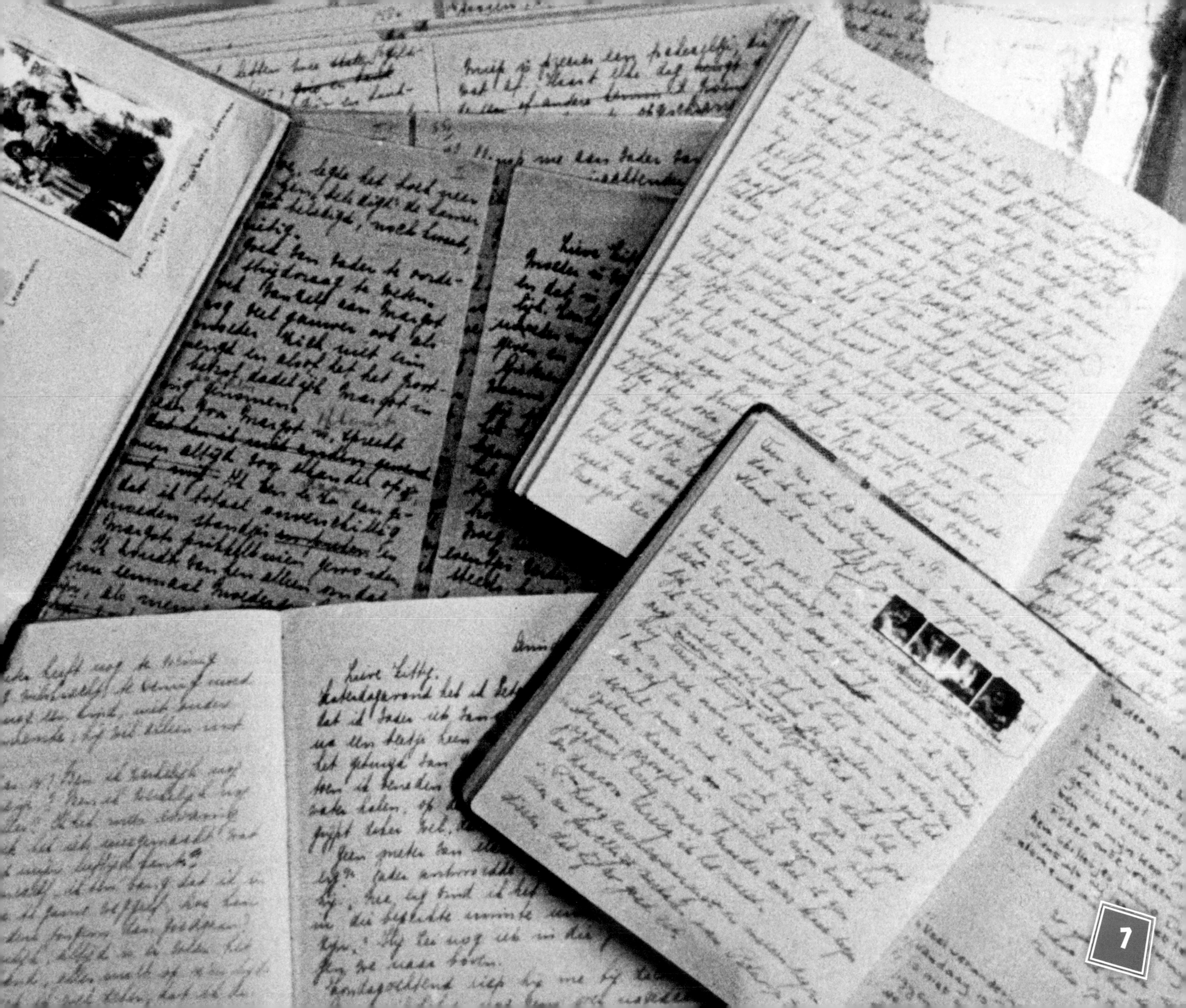

7

A primary source can be
a letter, a photo, a painting, a
diary, or a song. Anybody can
create one. Your family photos
are primary sources.

Families look at photos to see their
own history.

smile
LOVE
FRIENDS
laugh
happy
Family
good times
Love
Believe

Three Primary Sources

This primary source is a document. It is a piece of writing. It is called the Magna Carta. Signed in 1215 in England, it is seen as the basis for our laws.

The Magna Carta was signed by King John of England.

This primary source is a painting. It is a portrait of Benedict Arnold. He became famous as a traitor in the American Revolutionary War.

This portrait was painted in 1776 by English painter Thomas Hart.

A primary source can also be an object, such as a coin or a piece of clothing. Objects show us how people lived in the past.

Queen Elizabeth II of Great Britain wore this dress in 1953.

Primary or Secondary?

People use primary sources to create secondary ones. Some secondary sources are nonfiction books, articles, and encyclopedias.

Libraries are full of books, which are secondary sources.

Authors of secondary sources

tell about a time

in history they did not see.

They might write about what

happened 50 years ago.

This woman is reading about a time long ago.

If you really want to feel like a part of history, find a primary source. Go back to the moment. Then look, listen, and learn!

An archaeologist examines the remains of King Tut, who lived more than 3,000 years ago.

Activity: Primary Sources and Your Senses

Primary sources help us experience history through our five senses. We can hear sounds in a video. We can see an artist's creation in a painting. We can smell or taste food by following an old recipe. We can feel emotions by reading a diary or touching the tools of a famous inventor.

1. Look at the two primary sources on this page.

2. For each primary source, write the answers to these questions:

   What kind of primary source is this? (A document? An object? A picture?)

   Which senses does the primary source help you use? Why?

An instrument played by Mozart, a famous composer in the 1700s

An 1887 advertisement for land in the American Midwest

Northern Kansas.

AN INVITATION

IS HEREBY EXTENDED TO EVERYBODY DESIRING A CHOICE HOME IN THE

FINEST COUNTRY

IN THE WORLD,

TO VISIT THE PLACES

DESCRIBED IN THIS FOLDER

Glossary

archaeologist—a person who studies human history by digging up remains and objects

author—a person who creates a work of art

composer—the writer of a piece of music

document—a piece of paper that contains important information

encyclopedia—a book or website that gives information on subjects that are usually arranged in alphabetical order

original—something new and unusual; the first version of a work of art

primary source—a work of art made by someone who is part of history; primary sources can be documents, photos, videos, or objects

secondary source—an account of an event from someone who did not experience it firsthand

Read More

Hord, Colleen. *Writing a Research Paper. Hitting the Books: Skills for Reading, Writing, and Research*. Vero Beach, Fla.: Rourke Educational Media, 2014.

Manushkin, Fran. *Stick to the Facts, Katie: Writing a Research Paper with Katie Woo. Katie Woo, Star Writer*. North Mankato, Minn.: Picture Window Books, 2014.

Internet Sites

FactHound offers a safe, fun way to find Internet sites related to this book. All of the sites on FactHound have been researched by our staff.

Here's all you do:

Visit *www.facthound.com*

Type in this code: 9781491460504

Critical Thinking Using the Common Core

1. How are primary and secondary sources different? (Key Ideas and Details)

2. Look at the photos in this book. Which primary source would help you study something that interests you? (Integration of Knowledge and Ideas)

Index

Word Count: 233
Grade: 1
Early-Intervention Level: 20